*Miracles &*

Mortifications

*Winner of the 2001*
*James Laughlin Award*
*of The Academy of American Poets*

The James Laughlin Award is given to commend and support a poet's second book. The only award of its kind in the United States, it is named in honor of the poet and publisher James Laughlin (1914-1997), who founded New Directions in 1936. The award is endowed by a gift to The Academy of American Poets from the Drue Heinz Trust.

Judges for 2001

Daniel Hall
Campbell McGrath
Marilyn Nelson

# Miracles & Mortifications

*Miracles* & Mortifications

prose poems by

## Peter Johnson

4/7/07

For GEORGE

HOPE YOU ENJOY
THESE JOURNEYS.

Peter

Peter John

## Acknowledgments

*The American Poetry Review:* "Departure," "Neanderthal," "Queen Hatshepsut,"
  "Socrates," "Nero," "Attila," "Charlemagne," "Monastic," "Marco Polo,"
  and "Peter the Hermit"
*Alembic:* "Samuel Johnson," "Costa Rica," "Tokyo," and "Greenland"
*Barnabe Mt. Review:* "Chichén Itzá"
*Colorado Review:* "Paris"
*Epoch:* "Fiesole," "Rio," "Barcelona," and "Provincetown"
*key satch(el):* "Joan of Arc," "Nostradamus," and "Johannes Kepler"
*Luna:* "Cairo" and "Sarajevo"

*Acknowledgments continue on page 59*

Publication of this book was made possible, in part, by grants from the National Endowment for the Arts and with public funds from the New York State Council on the Arts, a State Agency.

Printed and bound in the United States of America

Libary of Congress Cataloging-in-Publication Data

Johnson, Peter, 1951-
    Miracles & Mortifications : prose poems / by Peter Johnson
        p. cm.
    ISBN 1-893996-18-2 (alk. paper)
        I. Title: Miracles and Mortifications. II. Title
    PS3560.O3827 M67 2001
    811'.54--dc21                                                    2001026728

Published by
White Pine Press
P.O. Box 236, Buffalo, New York 14201

*for Genevieve and Kurt*

# Table of Contents: Part I

*Travels with Gigi*

# Table of Contents: Part II

*Travels with Oedipus*

# Part I

*Travels with Gigi*

Love is the inborn suffering derived from the sight of and excessive meditation upon the beauty of the opposite sex, which causes each one to wish above all things the embraces of the other and by common desire to carry out all of love's precepts in the other's embrace.

That love is suffering is easy to see, for before love becomes equally balanced on both sides there is no torment greater, since the lover is always in fear that his love may not gain its desire and that he is wasting his efforts. . . . To tell the truth, no one can number the fears of one single lover.

—Andreas Capellanus, *The Art of Courtly Love*

Madame Bovary, c'est moi.

—Gustave Flaubert

# Home

Nighttime. I'm hitched to a machine, nursing a noun, tapping a verb on its shoulder, apposing appositives. Moments earlier, I was cruising the Internet, taping, then dancing to, national anthems of my favorite countries. "We never go anywhere," I complained, maneuvering colored tacks around my wall-sized atlas. My vertebra had cracked; that's what happened. Then it healed; now just an incredible longing for travel. This morning, tiny children hung upside down from damp branches of our dogwood tree, whispering *baby, baby, baby*. A premonition? A warning? Sure feels like a baby's brewing, someone to keep company with our tow-headed boy asleep in his prince-sized bed. Burnt popcorn! Pigeons shitting on the patio! Insatiability of tomato worms! This is "home." But also our Treasure Island bedsheets, with an ancient map of someone's tropical paradise. It looks like a board game. "Gigi, I beg you to come closer." And your response? "Don't call me that." It's a childhood nickname, but one that stuck . . . Bedtime, all bashfulness banished. Quiet, save the croaking of a few insomniac crickets and the roar of a Harley. Tonight we'll tumble down Love's dark hole, a trail of responsibilities, like breadcrumbs, behind us. "Set the bed for vibrate," I whisper, wondering who'll make the first move.

# Paris

A white poodle named Gigi. A fingernail red as the fire breather's face, red as my sparrow's neck, which you sometimes touch. Louis XIV boasted, "I am the State." Rimbaud, "JE est un autre." But I respond, "Je ne comprend pas." To come so far and stumble over a poodle named Gigi beneath an ancient fountain, beneath a tarnished Greek statue—his beard of seaweed, his baton and chiseled smirk. Impossible to be so sad beside this school of oversized goldfish and a poodle named Gigi. "Dear fated name!" So accustomed to miracles was Abelard, yet humbled by the pale of Eloisa's shoulders, her oval mouth, as I am also. How my Gigi-magician pulls silk panties from our hotel dresser, like colored tissues from a fancy box. How she mocks my cotton pajamas until I yell in protest, "Forehead," or "Foreskin."

This white poodle named Gigi, by a fountain, begging for a bone.

To whom shall I give it?

# London

Our down comforter discomfited, your cheeks complementary, like one white sun passing its light to another. I want to leap back into your pouch, bashful as fledgling corn. But there's work to be done. My white shirt and striped tie, my thin, black belt and shiny shoes that balance raindrops like newly-waxed cars. I'll wear these. I'll befriend women with bread batter on their hands, women who reek of beer. You'll be jealous, but consoled, as always, by your opulent ear lobes, with which you toy, endlessly. Are you sleeping or mad? Rescue me from the sting of after-shave, the certainty of slapping myself awake. A sign perhaps, show me, a gesture or jester to soothe.

I stroke your cheek, and your cruel finger responds—points to a doorway that has no door.

# Rio

"Scrimmaging with a fat-calved bossa novan," was how it came to me in this far-off rainy country, delivered, as it was, by a hairy-knuckled, limey poet with heavily endowed pockets and alligator cowboy boots. What a stinker! I was watching the telly, waiting for a response from the Lithuanian Writer's Colony, which promised me time for introspection and sexual group-groping in a medieval castle. I say I was watching the kidney pie bake in the oven, eyeing the peasants in our Dutch miniature as they glanced up from their gruel. I was frozen in that long-drawn-out "how" we call love. So take a bird to Rio, I thought, find out who's been undressing the corpse, and poof!, like magic, my stewardess and peanut snack arrived. I opened my notorious notebook, amused myself, lyrically. I raved, I wrote, I roved between fine gray lines, anticipating that neuter nation promised in the brochure, though smart enough not to trust prophets, poets, or travel agents, and love, well, when it speaks in the first person, you better be listening. I strove for a mind-set parallel to yours, I whispered your mantras "Hello" and "Goodbye." I sought you in the infamous *favelas* with their terminally still streets. Was sent this way, that way, driven by the memory of our furious five years of amazing starts and finishes. But it was worth it when drenched, at last, in the terrible narcolepsy of each other's arms, we watched from our hotel window as peasants pilgrimaged to the outstretched arms of a giant holy statue. They were chanting, "We, We, We," but the position of our bodies suggested the "I's" had won the day.

# Costa Rica

Whatever Gigi wants, Gigi gets. This time it's the day-flying, cyanide-filled moth, *Urania ripheus,* infamous for copulating with different species. "Ugh! Yuk! There's a bug, squash it," I tease, not wanting to burst from my hammock-cocoon. I wanted to help but had promised our host, René, that I'd clean the poison frog garden. Then I remembered this aphorism: "Universal hostility and fear toward a species are the products of ignorance." I also remembered Gigi's promise of a juicy love-bite to be given beneath a huge banana tree near the forking paths . . . Long-curved leaves the size of scimitars, bright green spikes of plantains, and a white-skinned woman, her bare breasts barely the size of serpent eggs, her dark eyebrows alert, like two facing centipedes. I'm adjusting my loincloth, then waving my butterfly net made from a clothes hanger and the thinnest of Gigi's panties. "Leaping lepidoptera. I got one." Two ear-sized wings fringed with golden hair, its underside red and veined like a tiny heart. Drip drop, drip drop. Then naked we lie beneath our banana tree, bold as two mottled stink bugs. I hold the moth between my fingers, then let go. "Erotic things occur in the rain," Gigi whispers, about to sink her teeth into my neck.

# Provincetown

We laughed about the pine tree laying its eggs, the blue fright wig I
bought last Halloween, then a little wine, and a little more. The bed next
door began creaking a foreign, same-sex language. I was reading a thin
book wherein a fat lady wrestles with nouns. A book taking sixty years
to flower. Later, we stumbled into a tree-shaded courtyard where white
marble lions drank from an albatross' basin. We had run out of booze,
and I kept having to pee. "So go one last time," and "Okay, I will." The
mean mosaic of the courtyard floor was making me dizzy, anyway. Off-
season, the narrow streets were barren, the frigid, salt air from another
century when wreckers scoured the beaches for boxes and barrels.
"Gigi," I said, "in the fall the cows here often feed on cods' heads! Did
you know that?" "And capybaras have webbed feet and are excellent
swimmers," she replied, understanding my foreplay. We would have
continued if not for a large poster of a petrified, Amazonian face
eyeballing us from a tarred telephone pole. "The Fat Bitch Is Back," the
poster announced. And we had to believe it, suddenly confronted by a
woman dressed like a bird cage, and another like an umbrella. Really
nice people, though, in spite of their cheap costumes. "Are we hungry
yet? Are we downright famished?" Gigi nodded, knowing a loss is not a
great loss, and that the liquor stores didn't close until midnight.

# Geneva

Banished from one writer's colony for blowing the whistle on a certain Southern plagiarist, this is true. Booed at The Great Poetry Slam—true again. Not to mention a certain liaison with a long-stemmed reference librarian who slashed Gigi with a letter opener for reading our love letters. This time, they promised we'd be "drunken, expatriate writers" for two weeks, and that the roast beef sandwiches would be juicy. Just clean tables and look intelligent, write a few poems now and then. So I grew a handlebar moustache to mimic the horny social-activist-poet who tried to skim the skin with Gigi while she served the sorbet. He had seen her play tennis and was, as he said, "overhauled by her overhand." I continued to clean the antique wooden tables of lettuce scraps and garbanzo beans, thinking of a good place to hide Gigi's racket. Fortunately, we were saved by a telegram announcing that I had won "The-Man-Least-In-Touch-With-His-Feminine-Side Contest." A strange contest indeed, especially since I didn't enter it. And the reward? Fifty dollars and two weeks in Geneva to study with the author of the trilogy *He, She, It*—a man steeped in *paternalia,* who enigmatically fingered his fly, asking over and over, "Who are you really, La-La Boy?" In a dimly lit room, he tightened leather straps around my wrists, tied a rooster to my desk and ordered it to peck out my eyes. But the rooster was really a French poet who'd been transformed into a rooster for sticking pins into chickens for the fun of it. The rooster-poet balked. "Who are you really?" my tormentor demanded, his white head looking as if it had just been fetched from the freezer, his almond-shaped hands quivering. *Je suis Gigi,* is what came to me, and *"Je suis Gigi,"* is what I said. As if on cue, her ancient, wooden racket came crashing through my blackened window, signifying both triumph and rescue . . . Later, a stiff wind off Lake Geneva, Gigi stroking my hair, feeding me tiny chocolates stolen from a local confectionary. I'm staring into a white, head-shaped cloud, my universe running in reverse, my own head haunted by the vision of a half-stitched Frankenstein, searching the mountainside for his father. An odd thought, if not for the insight of our rooster-poet, who keeps reciting in impeccable French: "Even the dumbest dreams can astound us."

# Cairo

Morning proclaimed by the cry of a car alarm and the whine of a sales-man on the hotel cable TV. You are imitating the goddess of pouting, I'm waving my worthless magic wand. A boat ride down the Nile seems in order, far from the hoarse laughter of the sea and last night's flirtatious waiter who swore he spoke French after being hit by a Yellow Cab. You said he had the "upper body of an archangel." I'll remember that. "We'll go as far as the third cataract, then turn around when the first skull presents itself," I say to cheer you up. On board, I lecture passengers, explain, "This is a land of unassisted patricides and many stunted shrubs and bamboos." I have them really confused until the head of a hip-popotamus appears off the starboard bow, driving home the fear of being eaten. On shore, we separate from the pack and wander into the desert. "The touch of your breast," I whisper, "could soften a stone." But there are no stones, so I offer my worthless cheek. Rebuked, I stare lovingly at a burning bush, pretending it's your face. I take solace in the kindred nightmares we shared last night, knowing we may never make it back, grounded by the head butt of that angry hippo. What luck! Was it because I ordered "Item 666" from the Home Shopping Channel this morning, or just our need to escape and destroy everything over and over again? "Love's funny like that," you say, watching our wet, disheveled companions mount a distant dune.

# Moscow

The old geezer from Gîza freezing his butt off downstairs. I'm twisting the corners of my moustache, which itself is Bolshevik blood-red. He's made his obsessive trip for nothing, doesn't even know how to dress in the cold. What a nail-biter! You've changed your name to Alexandra, your feet a mess of scar tissue, your toe shoes stained with blood. You eat only ice cream and just-thawed pot pies. But your impresario, Yuri, adores you, says you'd be his best bare-breaster if you laid off the sweets and took private showers with the local thugs . . . Time for a private pas de deux, so I pour us some vodka, then lie on my stomach, awaiting your heart-shaped footprints on the pale canvas of my back. Will we ever forget last night's tattered tutu or your grand jeté into a pool of red Jell-O? . . . We're off again, racing past tchotchke shops and broken-down trucks of cabbage and beets in a limousine driven by our Mongol bodyguard who scatters peasants with his long leather whip. Much later, admirers pelt you with petals from a makeshift balcony, and you shout, "I will return and I will be millions"—a shameful theft of language, but it works, especially on the old geezer who's followed us home in his black Mercedes. In the morning, the police find him floating in the Moskva, clutching his pet skull of Rasputin, the Mongol's whip wrapped around his neck. "Don't you think it's time for a change?" I ask. "Something more tear-worthy?" But you're fidgeting with your leather tassels, trying desperately to tame a banana split.

# Fiesole

Intrigues are exhausting, so are pets and professors, photographers and poets. It's a long walk to the orange groves, especially when I was ordered to stay home. This time, Gigi clothed in little besides a fishnet tank top and a pair of sky-blue running shoes. Brand new shoes, the gel still ungelled. Shoes attached to her ankles, her ankles to her calves, her calves to her thighs—parts poeticized by this skinny Polish photographer in black, skin-tight Levis who could pass for a child, except for the scar across his forehead and missing left thumb. Cowering behind a mossy boulder, I look and listen: "A little kick this time," he laughs, and Gigi complies, awakening a squadron of fruit flies. It's early, still damp, the dew frozen on branches and orange blossoms, which look like fancy glass-blown earrings. Now he tells her to shed the tank top, and I think, *It's time for Rome. Yes!* I have the urge to go Roman, to order broad-shouldered, Amazonian slaves to lug ice from nearby mountains and blend it with honey and fruit juices. Then I'll behead them. But we're not in Rome; just a cloud of fruit flies, and Gigi, bare-naked in her sky-blue running shoes. I swear it!

# Oslo

On my table, a glass half-empty. On yours, a lace bra, childlike simplicity. You're reading to me: "Once upon a time there was a goody who had seven hungry bairns." Words like these have brought us here, chasing the Peace Prize of a sickly inventor, as if we can unbury his dead with our own big boom. Personally, I'd rather unsheathe and wax down the cross-country skis. You can smell fish even with the windows closed, and the groaning of the grain elevators is deafening. "Speak louder to me, mother dear. Give me a bit of pancake, I am so hungry." What we need is a fire in a cabin on some vast white plain, far from blasting caps and nitroglycerin. A place where I can hide my medal and citation. Walking down Karl Johansgate past the Royal Palace, I think of the great fire of 1624 and listen to my boots crunch on dry snow—like Danes slashing Celts with very sharp swords. You pat me on the head and say, "Oh, darling, pretty, good, nice, clever, sweet darling." And the weather tomorrow? "Mostly crummy." Alfred Nobel never married but befriended Bertha Kinsky, one of the world's leading pacifists. You said I would have been the greatest humanitarian of my generation if I didn't sleep so much.

# Greenland

Icebergs the size of great ships melting in a blue fiord; large stones undisturbed for centuries; white-haired grandmothers in a hot spring, their heads bobbing like the flared nostrils of hippopotami a thousand miles away. Permanence. Eskimo strength, suckled by the blood of Eric the Red. You hear that, Gigi? Permanence. Predictability—like the small, stoic potatoes this cold earth gives up. Tough, like these grandmothers who won't leave earth when they die; instead expire on arctic boulders, where caught by moonlight, they flap like a catch of capelin. In the morning, just a pack of seals breathing heavily in a shine of water as black as love. And why are we here? Everyone together: Because in Notre Dame, Gigi made a pass at her wrist with a razor and called me her "quasi-Quasimodo," displaying a cracked picture to prove it. I blamed it on a little French girl's behind and two fish swimming in opposite directions. But, by God, I took responsibility . . . I'm on my way to her cabin, carrying a bottle of Australian wine and a bag of Cheetos, my boots battling a moat of tundra vegetation. Gigi's in a lamp-lit window, pounding brown dough into phallic shapes, then massaging them with a cube of white butter. "Now sleeps the crimson petal, now the white," I sigh, which somehow consoles me. And also the fact that Greenland has no trees. Nowhere for an anxious lover to hang himself. No trees, few vegetables, just rocks. Permanence. Stick-to-itiveness. So I leave, dragging my long tale of sins behind me.  Later, I cover myself with seal skins, read out loud in my canvas cot. It's a little book of love poems, one box-shaped, like a window, through which a sandy coast appears, tall cypresses swaying like showgirls, beckoning.

On Bastille Day in Notre Dame, Gigi parted her thickly painted lips and whispered to an astonished art historian, "I love to watch naked men play."

I tell you, comments like that drive me crazy.

# Palm Springs

Maxing out stolen credit cards, we know a week from now they'll never find us. We're out to prove Love has no landlord—that is, you can't hit a moving target. But how to reckon these peculiarities: a fat, black spider dangling from our obligatory fake chandelier; the soft, caterpillar moustache of our blondie-boy pool attendant; and a pack of paparazzi downing shots as two Mexicans are clubbed senseless on TV. Now this is American history! Gigi's fashioning her toothbrush into a skeleton key. I'm hardening my belly to look like the baroque bread board I spied in the souvenir shop. Later, I loiter around the porcelain dog bar with a bow-tied poodle dressed like a Vanderbilt, his owner's herringbone, golden necklace awash on her breast. Try to be friendly, I think, offering to interpret her surgical chart—face-lifts, tummy tucks. "You'd make a good pet," she purrs, blaming her flirtation on a gene she inherited for ass-biting, passed down from one anxious countess to another. If I just had my golf clubs, I'd stay here forever. What a place, where women come dripping out of pools, slick as seals, their empty eye sockets bathed in sunlight, their calf muscles hardening like pears. I could get rejuveniled here. But don't tell Gigi, who's just returned with the loot and a bottle of imported Scotch . . . A little ice, some natural darkness, and a moon frozen in the sky like a pale Frisbee. I tell her, "Receiving a stolen gift is naughty but erotic," then accept the pen she gives me with its skin of hardest opal. Tonight a team of cosmonauts passes quietly overhead. In the morning, we try to escape from each other's grip, but the bedroom mirror hardens us.

# Bombay

*Namaste!* By the laws of Love Fanaticism, I should be angry, but let us first consider what Love is. You say it's like facing a different dictator every night, or like a still life without the banana. I deny this accusation, in spite of the young rajah's supporting testimony. How to trust this shrimp, anyway, his heart so fragile he collapsed while watching you suck mercilessly on a pomegranate. Agitated he was, his mantra squawking like a parrot mistaken for a clay pigeon. You could hear his loin-sigh all the way to New Delhi. Then he disappeared, his henchmen breaking down our door, expecting to discover him wedged between your breasts. Fortunately, they missed the erotic pictures we scratched on odd bits of wall space, or it would have been my head, so to speak. All this trouble because we had run out of drugs, and I thought the travel agent had said, "An ideal place for medication." The sheen from her long painted fingernails still haunts me, as we race through Bombay, wrapped in brightly colored blankets. It's the time of *Holi,* when revelers douse each other with fine-colored powder and water. "Dive into the crowd," I yell, and we're carried far from these loveless British buildings, far from the rajah's artificial leg and the half-formed beggars who line the causeway, mumbling, *Namaste! Namaste!* . . . Weeks later, hundreds of miles away, we watch the sacred rats of Karai Ma scurry across a marble courtyard. Here it is written that dead poets return as rats, dead rats as poets. "Everything as it should be," you say, without the slightest hint of anger.

# Barcelona

Moonlight softens the hardwood floor. A wind-blown, hundred-year-old dust ball scurries under the bed. And a fat black spider—our love child—awakens; its legs bloom, its web shimmers, like lace panties stretched tightly and held up to the sun. We are resting after a day of massaging my moods. "Happy love has no history," I whisper. But tonight that's hard to believe. Annoyed by the chi-chi shops and capitalists speaking Catalonian into their cellular phones, we went to the cathedral to view St. Eulalia's crypt. It was very quiet, and I said I remember nothing until the age of forty-one when I saw you step out of an elevator. Perhaps that's why you are so quiet tonight, naked except for a collar of Majorcan pearls. "If you come to Barcelona," I would tell tourists, "you will see this and you will discover that, and you will find my Gigi kneeling before the crypt of St. Eulalia. And you will think, *Someone should tell their stories; someone should tell them they are beautiful.*"

# Hong Kong

If we wrestle, it should be with honor. That's what I say. You wanted to go to Milan to buy a hat, but they needed a blond for their thick-haired chop-chop hero, so I watched you kiss him over and over again until you got it right. Kisses can be hard like drops of water, or soft as smoke rings. In the afternoon, I went looking for snakes and watched Chinese characters bleed on buildings. I had expected to find mills that never lacked for grain, fat country rats holding high carnival. But instead, towers of concrete scraping the sky and costumes designed by once-upon-a-time French aristocrats. It makes me want to return to my hobbit hole. *Patience, patience,* then a patch of sky wounded by the blades of a helicopter—enter our heroine, my Gigi, and her chop-chop guy. He's dragging her by the hand through a crowd of stand-ins, until I wrestle him to ground. Much yapping, mostly in French. A few brush burns on Mr. Chop-chop, and a smile from Gigi. In the morning I awake to the buzz of a cockroach the size of a paper airplane, Gigi already on the run.

# Tex-Mex

"Everything in this world passes, but Love will last forever." If this is true, then where is my Gigi this morning? I am naked, half-embalmed, like a worm at the bottom of a brown bottle, a certain Black-eyed Susan curled around my leg, only the sound of my palomino weeping in the prairie grass. My battery is dead, my cactus has growing pains . . . We were searching for the Old Dutchman's mine, our guide Buck a consummate rough rider in every kind of saddle. Joe the Bad and Jim the Ugly brought up the rear. "Call me Blue or Coyote," I drawled, which made Gigi laugh. Or was it my Styrofoam pith helmet with the smiley-face decal on front? "We'll be breaking virgin territory," Buck grunted, but all I saw was a huge pyramid of cast-off microwave ovens. The day wore on, the sun dragging it westward like a withered foot. We shot a few elk and wild pigs, milked some rattlesnakes. At the hoedown at Apache Jack's, we shared campfire stories. "I had a cheesy childhood," I began, "one with many holes in it, and a heavy Thing, a Thing like the last tree left standing so you can build a house around it." "When you're done, Stretch," Buck said, opening a large, brown bottle of mescal, "can you pass the beans?" And what do I remember? The raw outline of a covered wagon branded on Buck's forearm, his red hair bristling like porcupine quills, then bushwhacked I was by a certain Black-eyed Susan, whose snoring now seems as cruel as hunger—the price to pay for going home with the wrong Gigi.

# Scotland

We started out highbrow, riding the Royal Scotsman, curling through a countryside chiseled by glaciers, guests of ancient, overfed aristocrats whose mug shots I spied on a chipped Chippendale desk in London. They thought Gigi a historian of porcelain, me a connoisseur of cashmere. But before their tea had cooled, I ended up in the caboose scraping horns with a certain chambermaid. Next thing I know I'm wandering the woodlands, a Highlander, tossing the caper against a MacDougal with a sheep's nose and peat-stained hands. "It's all my life I wanted to lay siege to a certain Gigi," he bleats, though he just met her an hour before. Fortunately, he couldn't swim, so we headed for a firth, then pitched a tent near a small loch. So romantic camping out: an apricot sunset, rosy campfire, with the hope of a giant serpent offshore. Gigi's roasting marshmallows, imagining toilet seats nailed down by little feminine hammers. "It's the water makes me think of it," she laughs. So I play along, call myself Upright John, whack her on her bare fanny with my wooden spoon. Splash, splash! Nessie coiling her heroic shoulders? Or just some twisted plant surfacing? Moonlight creates this lacuna, this gap just large enough to tease us, large enough to make us doubt. "Gigi," I say, approaching this apparition, heroically adjusting my kilt, "all this commotion makes me seriously worried."

# Transylvania

I'm singeing my toenails, tacking a pig's head above the doorjamb, throwing a shoe onto the fire. Not even the eggplant stuffed with force-meat, the plum brandy, or rum balls the size of walnuts can quiet my insides. We were searching for the Perfect Red, so embarked on a hemoglobular journey into the horseshoe of the Carpathians. *Stegoica,* the peasants called you, peppering us with paprika and sour cherries, driving us into the forest. Lost until we came upon a carrot-topped cadaver with a sheeplike schnoz, who smelled worse than cooked cabbage. He asked you to ride with him, displaying a movable horn on his saddle, which made me clench the hilt of my anxious sword. But we had to follow, enticed by the promise of a soft bed and crimson pillows. He changed your name to Gigushka, mine to Gyorgy. "Did you know, Gigushka," he said, "corpses are smaller than living bodies?" Why didn't you flinch? Then at daybreak he ordered us to gather buckets of rasp-berries and to search for a virgin riding a black virgin stallion. So when did the violation occur? Where is that stink bomb, Hungarian hedgehog now? "I shall get a steam launch and follow him," is what I said, but am now afeard to leave this house. Instead, I trace puncture marks on your neck, stare into your zombie eyes, watch time tick off on a tooth-shaped bedroom clock. At night, I listen to insomniac crickets chant his name: *Nosferatu! Nosferatu!* In the shape of a toad, in the shape of a cockroach, he'll return for his Gigushka. I know this, so practice waving a large Celtic cross, fashioned from potato candy and dried goulash. I'll sever his head, by God, come raging at him like a burning haystack on a pitchfork. I'll hemoflagellate him.

# Berlin

These are a Grimm people, in spite of their hi-ho metal picks. Each one takes a whack at the wall while children cheer, riding their fathers' shoulders through a gate previously leading to nowhere. Heal me, Doctor Gigi! Who else would have opened a New Age shop at this moment? *A Created Thing,* you call it, after Leibniz, that ass-kisser. "Thanks a lot. Yeah, yeah, yeah." And another thing, "I don't like belonging to someone else's nightmare. . . ." I'm face down on a cot, staring through a head-sized opening at a poster of the ocean; I'm listening to a tape of seagulls squawking, waves lapping on shore. "Call me Iron Hans," I say, recalling your lecture last night on quartz penetrators. What a crystal, indeed! Yesterday, you massaged my temples, said I had the forehead of an imbecile who would live long; you charted the moles on my back with patchouli oil. But it's the metal band around my heart that needs breaking. "Repeat after me," you say, kneading my neck with your unforgiving knuckles: "All is a plenum, and in the plenum every motion has an effect upon distant bodies in proportion to their distance. . . ."

Yeah, yeah, yeah. Thanks a lot.

# Cannes

A poached egg without the pocket, embarrassed before the tongue's eye. Have you ever felt like that? Cagey croissant bars, two baby shrimp cavorting on a bed of artichokes, floating houses, flying fish, and sleek limousines squatting in front of Belle Epoch hotels—a splendid cubist landscape, yet here we are encamped on a beach in moth-eaten sleeping bags. In this take, Gigi's a nun. Not like a nun, but a real one—at least in her mind. "Nun, the feminine of *nonnus*—old man." We're talking bodily integrity, here! Virginity! What a laugh. I was up early, sucking on my kava kava Think! Bar, drawing a huge smiley face on our hotel ceiling with a piece of lipstick tied to the tip of a bamboo pole. Then I decided to buy a newspaper. Came back to a certain Gigi sitting upright in bed, wearing her plum edible panties and a white T-shirt emblazoned with the image of Sean Penn. She was aglow, people, that's a fact. Later she explained:

> He appeared on the red wallpaper! My flesh fell to the floor. I was stripped by lightning! . . . What beauty! What elegance and sweetness! His shoulders, his bearing! Such a peaceful shining face!

Who was I to doubt, though there was something familiar about this ecstasy. And it came to pass . . . Gigi and I giving alms, warning the infidels to heal themselves, making pilgrimages to the cell of The Man in the Iron Mask—all the time my orchids swelling beneath my cassock, unable to look away from the near-espresso tans of half-naked starlets and hangers-on. "According to *A New Catholic Dictionary*," I warned, "ecstasies as a rule do not last long." But she'd have none of it. And my last image of these days? Waking on the beach, a morning sea breeze toying with Sister Gigi's white cotton robe, her Holiness rolling onto her side, and, like a good Christian, turning a pale cheek. A miracle? An optical illusion? No, just a tattoo of winged old St. Michael, waving his shiny, righteous sword in my face, his long blond, Nordic locks flaming behind him.

# Tokyo

They were looking for "The New Vagina Girl." It wasn't like it sounded, Mr. Cold-Under-the-Collar explained. Just two weeks, some light chores, smile a lot. Hadn't we heard this before, Gigi? Men, men, men, this one with a head as hard and hairless as a hand grenade, driven by that great snow-coned breast threatening to spill its heat into the city. Oh where, oh where is my Gigi today? I sing, watching blurred pornographic movies on late-night TV. Sometimes I look out the window, see men in dark blue suits and crewcuts stumbling out of clubs. I consider seppuku with a Ginsu knife, shove miniature sushi rolls into each ear, then drift into a saki-induced sleep. In the morning, breakfast arrives: a piece of bluefin tuna dressed with lotus seed paste and . . . what? It's a message, gentle reader: "I have tasted salt water from the dimples of Gigi's back. Meet us at midnight on the roof of Mitsukoshi's. . . ." Nighttime, a few helicopters passing overhead, the city cloaked in neon, Gigi and Mr. Cold-Under-the-Collar no more than fifty feet away. She's done up like a geisha, reciting poetry, banging a sick tune on a funny-looking banjo. But she can't fool me. "Liberty for all!" I shout, charging her bodyguard, a bald sumo wrestler, who's squatting as if to give birth.

# Sydney

The universe expands, we feel its pull, its tug . . . The day awakens, brimming with brawn. We're crooked, my Gigi-girl and me, that is, slipped from our moorings. I mean, hungover. Consider last night's adventure at the Wombat Bar and Grill, our Captain balancing a tinny of beer on his bare belly, farting like a Piper Cub. Was this the great shark hunter? The man who rode six-hundred-pound turtles? Who broke a swamp fever by clinging to the body of a dead buffalo? Who kept a collection of exotic monkeys in his cellar? "Bunga, bunga, who's got the bunga," Gigi laughs, showing a bit of thigh through her straw skirt. "For an ordinary couple to have extraordinary sex," is what she really wanted—thus a tooth extracted from a great white shark captured at dusk, "then pulverized," she said, "stirred in a glass of tepid kiwi juice." I wanted a damp terry-cloth towel to wrap around my aching head, but, as it was written, "The day awakens, brimming with brawn. . . ." Three mates on board, all with identical blond moustaches, as if hatched from the same pouch. The Captain's donning his sharkskin hat, and, at long last, a glimpse of his famous webbed feet. "G'day," he says, squinting toward the horizon through a pair of leathery eyelids. "G'day, Bonza," we reply. What can I say, mates? A long day, the ocean turning blood-red for the sake of love. Our return, the Captain's small craft knocking on the harbor's dimwitted door. The fog horn weeping like a hero. And not to forget that blood-stained shark's tooth buried deep in a damp pocket of Gigi's bra—as beautiful and absurd as any glass slipper.

# Chichén Itzá

"Love preserved by destruction," our guide says. I sure know what that
means, as we peer into a rocky sinkhole where Mayan virgins were sac-
rificed. If I pushed you in, would it swallow you? . . . Another holiday,
we're naked on a hotel bed; outside, Spanish aristocrats in hiding, Indian
peasants chasing a huge wooden wagon down the street bearing an
equally huge pig, itself dressed like a Spanish aristocrat. They're whipping
the poor thing. Meanwhile, you're scratching my back with a handful of
bougainvillea, while I carve a cross into the dark brown icing of my
birthday cake. Another year gone, and where's the excitement? Not even
a fat check from the writer's colony to keep us going . . . "Don Diego,"
I say to our guide, "have you seen my Gigi?" He points to a relief
sculpture—rows of skewered skulls, each with its own personality. To be
honest, I prefer the sinkhole: the rocky descent, cruel roots scraping our
bare backs, the infamous virgin pool, just now illuminated by a shaft of
blue light.

And the virgins?

"Bad things happen to good people," you smile, with all the sympathy
you can muster.

# New York

Night, New York all gussied up. So much to do, but we're afraid to go out. Calf brains, hair from a wolf's tail, snake bone, even bits of a human corpse—ritually laid out on our bed. Love potions, uncocked concoctions to ward off suitors. We're waiting for a giant ape. "Do I look boxy?" Gigi asks, eyeing her hips in the bedroom mirror. She's fashioning an ape-like man from sugar cubes, setting a pitcher of warm tea next to him. So why are we afraid? Has the young master lost his wits? It was my fault. Sick of puzzling over the lines on my palms, sick of diving into holy lakes, I went to find the tribe who invented zero. I mean, I was searching for The Secret. But we got lost in the jungle, then captured by hard-bellied, coffee-colored virgins, who smeared my body with resin and blew gold dust on me until I glistened from head to toe. Unfortunately, they were hitched to a giant ape, who himself fell hard for Gigi. He tried to hold her gently like a small banana, but bruised her egg-white thighs. "Unhand her," I yelled, reminding him of a basic, irrefutable Rule of Love: "Whatever nature forbids, Love is ashamed to accept." The last time we saw him he was wearing a giant, silly wreath of orchids around his head, trying to swat rescue helicopters. "He smelled worse than that vampire," Gigi says, dropping the sugar ape into the pitcher, watching him dissolve. Outside, small aircraft hover, then the rat-a-tat-tat of a machine gun, and a hairy digit of flesh fingering our hotel window. "Do you think he's come for my binoculars?" I laugh, then leap onto the love potions, rolling on my back like a puppy.

Next day, standing near a giant tabernacle of ashes, the ape's weepy tribal princess speaks to the press. "I would have taken him back with no arms or legs," she says, "even if he were a stump."

# Home

If there is no Gigi, there is still her name . . . To be sure, a long winter, but now a spring breeze, like a sigh, carries us to the edge of our sheets. Across the hall, a tow-headed boy moans, tumbling from one clumsy dream to another. Adolescence—rascality, pure rascality! Tempestuated, like the crocuses gazing up in a panic, all too aware of their short-term erections. They know a Big Idea is ajar, our trip tripped. It was all too exhausting, anyway—the hotels, the intrigues. Better to hunker down, mine the backyard mulch for anemic worms, go fishing. Or maybe lie still a moment, contemplate the scars on your feet, the ant-sized beauty mark on your bum. The mailman sighs when you open the front door in a silk kimono, I sigh when you open any door. I swear this before our sharp-beaked lovebirds just now awakening in their golden cage, exchanging necklaces crafted from the legs of a spider; before the sacred shield of Jean de Jean, hanging in our garage next to the bicycle rack; before my yang, growing warm, hard, steadfast. "See?" you laugh. "This is how you get into trouble." And, of course, you're right. But I fear our fairy tale is fading—friends coupling and uncoupling in various unseemly ways. So again I plead, "Speak louder to me, mother dear. A bit of pancake, please, I am so hungry," and you pat me on the head and reply, "Oh, darling, pretty, good, nice, clever, sweet darling. . . ."

# Part II

## *Travels with Oedipus*

I want a hero: an uncommon want,
    When every year and month sends forth a new one,
Till, after cloying the gazettes with cant,
    The age discovers he is not the true one:

—Lord Byron, *Don Juan*


—Still there is some good, said Candide.
—That may be, said Martin, but I don't know it.

—Voltaire, *Candide*

# Departure

A new year! Yet no jubilation. Just a need to invent a language without coordination—as sinister as the history of a slave ship . . . I'm arranging my plaster-cast figures of famous men; you're leafing through *The Marquis de Sade's Everyday Collection*. Earlier, we fought over a cheap poster of a starlet's buttocks. It was a cold afternoon, hard to think with all that yelling. "Make your bed!" "Turn off the light!" "Take down that poster." "Don't put out cigarettes on the lovebirds!" "Do I ask too much?" I yell, then hurl a soiled Q-tip in your direction. I've heard confession helps: I confess to being a creature of detours, to stealing monogrammed towels from swank hotels. I even accept the savage history of my middle finger. But not you, O dearest boy, with a mind as tiny as Napoleon's hat, unforgiving as a nutcracker—Ouch! You, with your gelled head, slick and shiny as a seal's behind. Confess! Unburden yourself! And your teenangel response? "The true Daddy is against all Daddies." Later, huddling on your bed, we dive into the manic-depressed gene pool of the family photo album, our rescue team of women stranded in the soft snow outside. The poster's down, the starlet's tanned buttocks shivering on the hardwood floor. On the blank space of wall, a circular opening forms. An invitation? An escape? . . .

# Neanderthal

A head-shaped cloud takes a bite out of this prehistoric sun. We're staring at the silent pubic bone of a long-dead ancestor, a spear sticking out of his fractured skull. If you just had more facial hair we wouldn't be so conspicuous. And those perfect teeth are bound to piss them off. I remember this: "Some Neanderthals would suck brains from the skulls of their enemies." So tread lightly, my boy, blend in. We'll dust ourselves with clay and fossilized feces, fashion a tool driven by a concept, something to blow their little minds. They'll think we're gods with our little heads and big ideas. Or maybe we'll interbreed, give future bone-diggers something to ponder . . . Nearby, the sound of pee spraying the outside wall of our tiny cave. Peer over a boulder, and there he is: *Homo sapiens neanderthalensis*—squat and hairy-shouldered, with the exaggerated calves and biceps of a sumo wrestler, and a rocking gait, as if he just gave birth to a boulder. Ain't no pebble chopper, this one—instead, our future and our doom. So let's join the clan, spend days driving hyenas out of caves, nights waving lit branches overhead, dancing, as saggy-breasted females scratch out images of animals on a limestone wall. And our mission? To make everything noteworthy, of course—even this bear claw, even this pile of dung . . .

# Queen Hatshepsut

A fine mess you've gotten us into: surrounded by canopic jars of bodily organs, sharing space with a corpse—someone's minor deity—his gut as empty as a piñata; scrolls piled on top of each other like foot-long hot dogs; our flasks of Lebanon cedar gone bad. Why did you taunt the Poet Laureate of Deir el-Bahri? Sure, he had a cheap henna-dyed woolen wig. True, he'd stolen the high priest's leopard robe. Correct, he had an inflamed mole on his neck the size of a Hyksos hickey. Not to mention his poor sense of humor and false beard. Nothing to do but laugh when he proclaimed, with all the seriousness of Seti, "Men without breasts love war"—a line that wouldn't have gotten him a summer residency back home. But the Queen trusted him, and there were rumors: of hanky panky on the royal barge, of hunting trips in dog-drawn chariots, as terrified antelopes and gazelles raced in front, dodging arrows from the bow of the famous Queen. She liked you, too, made you walk around naked, powdered your cheeks with ochre, let you play with her sacred boomerang. You'd hide in the reeds while her servants scared up a few birds. I should have been concerned but was too busy drinking beer with the maidservants, wondering what creature possessed my heart in a previous life . . . Beautiful Hatshepsut, daughter of Thutmose and Aahmes, ravager of Punt, if only she knew where we were—buried deep in limestone and granite, glaring at each other over an ancient board game studded with catlike ebony and ivory figures. Too bad we don't know how to play!

# Socrates

Ah, the glory that was Greece! . . . excrement in the street and houses without windows. I wanted to teach you about Truth, which began as an idea rubbing its jaw against a rock but ended up too tiny to shed its skin. *Gnothi seauton!* (Know Thyself!) What a laugh! "Good means intelligent." "Virtue means wisdom." And what of Socrates? The bugger had a booger in his nose the first time we saw him; still they followed him, happy as hoplites. He seduced you, too, with endless questions, scraps of reasoning. Then the Games—the agora looking like home-coming weekend for dead philosophers, everyone talking in riddles. "Come home with your father," I said, and you answered, "What is father?" "Stop the nonsense," I ordered, and you asked, "What is its essential quality?" So I challenged Socrates to a wrestling match, but you took his place. Father and son. Mano a mano. What a testicular idea! . . . I'm leaning on a cypress, dressed in a loincloth, anointed with olive oil and dusted with white powder, my love handles and skinny legs a night-mare for any self-respecting bronze mirror. I'm led to a muddy pit, where you're squatting, all lathered and powdered like me. Lots of slapping, pushing, and sliding until I'm disqualified for face-biting. On my knees, blinded by a noonday sun, I'm barely able to spy Socrates as he approaches. "There's the story about a father," he laughs, "who swore he'd remain on earth as long as one son had need of him. Two days later, they found him hanging from an olive tree with an empty wine flask over his head."

# Nero

Coins were struck, inscriptions inscribed, monuments erected . . . *Ex gente Dimitiae duae familiae claruerunt*—I sing of Nero in a voice sweeter than that of Suetonius . . . Nero: wannabe poet and actor looking for a way to kill himself, haunted by the image of a poison mushroom the size of a Twinkie. Not exactly guilt, just too much inbreeding. "I dream of monkeys," he says. "I want to be buried with all my parts. I want to mount a woman concealed in the wooden image of Pasiphae. I want. . . ." He's disgusting; if he smiles at you one more time, I'll castrate him, break his favorite enema bottle over his head, the one shaped like a Grecian urn. I came here looking for a natural cure for baldness; I wanted you to see a real vestal virgin. Instead, peasants rioting because of the price of bread, and this red-haired Romeo who couldn't get a good grip on Agrippina. "The whole bunch of them are humorless," you say, then make fart noises by cupping a hand under your armpit and flapping your elbow up and down. Astonished, the Emperor recoils, punctures his neck with an ornate, ceremonial knife. "Time to go," I say, but first we finish his uneaten feast: roast parrot and sweet sauce, boiled tree fungi, and sow udders stuffed with salted sea urchins—all washed down with hot African sweet-wine. And as for the Zippo lighter you smuggled through time? Toss it into the hot tub, something for soothsayers and historians to think about.

# Attila

Attila the Hun, Whatsamaddawidyou! . . . This trip was your idea; I shouldn't have been surprised—years of broken bows and arrows, rubber knives and javelins I tossed into the garbage, plastic cap guns. Behold, conclusive proof that when two boys point swords at each other, someone gets hurt. We're camped near the Nischjava River, its banks strewn with human corpses, every other baby step a severed limb. "All this bad karma," I say, waving my finger at you. "All these pillaged and burnt monasteries, slain monks and virgins." Huns swarming like locusts, howling Scythian songs, warming pieces of venison between their thighs. "Want some?" the ferryman asks, stumbling toward his boat. He's drunk on kam, smells of ox and fish. He's waving a small knife, fashioned from the jawbone of a Roman. "No thanks, pal. Just had some boiled toe"—my best stab at Hunnic humor. All around *res gestae* germinating, traces of barbarian hair and skin. "Say goodnight," I say, then enter our sheepskin tent, collapse onto a large woolen mat. I allude to our conspiracy, "From the Latin *conspiro*, to breathe the same air." "Know your role," you warn, turning your back to me. Two days later, Attila sprawled on a bed of linen sheets; from its center a wooden pole sprouts, topped with a fresh Gallic head. A two-hundred-pound woman leaps up and down on his back, as if stamping out a fire. He never blinks, just rolls those sad Mongolian eyes. Later, he offers gifts: for you, an ornate handle from one of his whips; for me, a leather pillow stuffed with deer hair. The only time he smiles is when he calls me a "girlie girl." Humiliated, I nearly mention Bleda's story of him prancing through the moonlit woods, dressed in his wife's see-through silken robes, his toenails painted with ox blood. But the dismembered head makes me pause. I'm no Pope Leo, armed with the pitter patter of *Pater Noster.* I'm no hero. "Attila," the Roman historian Melodius reports, "while tying corpses into the fetal position with dried roots, was once heard to say, 'I am proud of my name. Whatever it is.'"

# Charlemagne

Who does not belong in this group: a. vassal; b. squire; c. scumsucking Saracen mounted on a pig? . . . Son, despite my sagging ass, the dithyrambic moaning of my spine, and my tongue's tantric rites, I've always wanted you to think me a Great Man. According to Sigmund, the Great Man exhibits traits of The Father. Let us ponder this remark, as we view the King Daddy of them all—his long white mane, thick and leathery neck. Corpulent, true, but strong and strong-willed, his broad chest protected by a jerkin made from the skins of otters and ermines. Both mac and Machiavellian, but with the heartbeat of a little girl. He entered the world straddling the hump of a rainbow; named twelve winds when before there were only four; and, embarrassed by his comeliness, prayed nightly to be given the head of a rat. Was it he who said, "No beauty without deformity," in a tone as reasonable as the number one? "No, it was not he," you interrupt, "and the hump of the rainbow story is also nonsense." You're here, my varlet, both to joot and to jouot. All night you lay awake listening to your pubic hair grow, fantasizing on veiled damsels, hot to unhorse Desiderata the Average, whose real name was Needlenose, just because he waved what he called his "enchanted lance" at the King's daughter. He arrives on horseback, accompanied by three Saracens—real angry guys with large black zeros on their backs, rusty chastity belts hanging from their saddles. "A real maiden cannot be made less," I offer in my Great Man voice, but you're not listening, your eyes flashing like an illuminated manuscript. Let the boys fight this one, let the squires squirm. I'm more interested in the golden hawk circling overhead with a pearl necklace dangling from its beak.

# Monastic

I wanted self-discipline without the pain, you to catch a glimpse of a noon-day devil. Monk, from *monachus*, "someone who lives alone. . . ." We were working in the fields when a raven passed overhead, dropping a loaf of bread on us. In it, an announcement of The Last Mortification Contest to be judged by the ghost of a hairy-chested fisherman. For one day, everyone would have the chance to be the Messiah. They paired us against a fat monk and his balding partner, famous for kissing stones, then lecturing them about responsibility. We began by eating little squares of bread sprinkled with the ashes of nuns, then prostrating ourselves 666 times to create a sense of irony. For our finale, I displayed dried palm leaves wrapped around my back like a python. You soaked the leaves in camel's blood, scraping away the thorns with a scalpel fashioned from the claw of a peacock. Everyone cheered, even the pagan with a placard proclaiming: "Mendicants Masticate." A protest? A direct order? It was hard to tell. And the winners? Weighing in at a mere 110 lbs. each, direct from the devil-infested deserts of Egypt, two ancient anchorites who conjured up a pride of lions and convinced them to dig their own graves "twenty baby fingers deep." It was the numerology that swayed the judge, who, amidst much psalm singing, presented the winners with a brand-new scourge and a bag of rock salt . . . Miracles and mortifications, all of them, just to prove that sin is a habit!

# Marco Polo

"The extraordinary! Like a moon rock, or the droppings of an exiled Venusian." "Venetian?" I ask, grabbing my little "Marco Polo, the ultimate in porcelain dolls. The wise and learned citizen of Venice." "Tap the back of his head," the instructions read, "and tiny black pearls shoot out his nose. Scratch his chin to the sound of four louts playing lutes. . . ." *Il milione.* What a trip—a ship of war, its bow guarded by slingers and bowmen, catapults and heaps of stone missiles, the constant blare of trumpets, the pounding of kettledrums. Heave ho! Heave ho! But at least no sorry-sack pirates or complaining crusaders. We bear oil from the tomb of Christ and an orange tree from Fiesole. Shall I tell you more? We sleep on hard, wooden benches, our dreams thick with the green ooze and weed of Venice and its foul-mouthed whores. Shall I tell you more? Of elephants wrapped in silk jock straps ornamented with gold filigree, of lions the size of gondolas. Of how I neglected to wear white leather slippers in the palace, or sneezed onto the Great Khan's food, or bumped into his flagon of mare's milk as it flew through the air at the nose-twitch of his favorite lama. "Silence!" you command, flanked by two silk-clad prostitutes, an imperial lion lapping fresh snails out of your hand. "My dad," you laugh, "some hotshot voyager." Next thing I know I'm basting the bottom of Khan's private ship with quicklime and tung oil, then given a month to travel by elephant and steal a strand from the beard of each dead Wise Man. And where are you now, my dearest boy? And where is my Marco? Shall I tell you more? . . .

# Peter the Hermit

The Higgins Museum—fresh from pinching coats of armor and instruments of torture, the odor of raw meat fresh in our nostrils, then home to the lovebirds who're squawking again. "Stuff them with bread crumbs and glue them to their swing," you suggest—no doubt a remnant of today's carnal outing. But lest you forget: "Every evil deed has a price. . . ." "Dieu Le Volt! Dieu Le Volt!" Weary, dehydrated, we're up to our necks in mud, trying to absorb its moisture. To wit, this host could use a good hosing down, not to mention a doctor—darts of Saracens clinging to us like a second skin. Lombards and lardasses slitting their horses' throats and drinking the blood, the smoke from Saladin's camp obscuring the sun. "It's like a Fellini movie," I say, "but without Italians." All this discomfort "Because," as the apostle writes, "He has laid down His life for us; and we ought to lay down our lives for the brethren. . . ." Peter the Hermit, surnamed Kiku Peter, appears in a woolen shirt reaching to his ankles; he's barefoot, followed by a dog with one ear. "Five hundred gold *besants* to the first man arriving at Constantinople," he announces, inadvertently stepping onto my mound of mud. "Did he say beeswax?" I ask, shaking the dirt from my ears. Through my inflamed eyeball, through the thin smoke, I spy a tongue of fire in the shape of a sword, the sword in the shape of a cross, then a nearby whisper: *My crusade is better than yours.*

# Joan of Arc

. . . and there she sat with her breasts pressing against the tightly laced tunic, her fettered legs flung carelessly in front of her, the opening between her tunic and hose revealing the flesh of her thighs as far as the sketchy strip of linen that was no more than a *cache-sexe*.

Whoof! A dramatization, for sure, but one capturing your boyish imagination . . . Jean la Pucelle! The Devil's Milkmaid! Armagnac Whore! Depends on your point of view. Just ask Cauchon, that crooked vessel of reason, only interested in who's getting The Treat, as dumb as a sack of flour. But we're not interested in Cauchon. We've come for her thigh—not the white light streaming from her eyes, nor the naked angel squatting on her left shoulder; not the chains on her neck and hands, nor the sacred bird nibbling squares of bread from her lap. Not even her scorched, holy heart, soon to be dragged along the bottom of the Seine. Let monks and historians chronicle these facts. It's her thigh we've come for, just a scrap of it—pearl-pale, creamy . . . Oh, Lordy!

# Nostradamus

An airplane's toilet tumbles toward earth. Predicted. A chicken squats and gives birth to a hailstone. Predicted, too. Why not? you ask, your neck weighed down with a blue crystal the size of a golf ball, a temporary tattoo of a half-moon on your cheek. Was that you I saw talking to a pea, picking nightcrawlers off the sidewalk? I liked you better when you were nasty. Look! there's gouty Nostradamus, all grim-faced, as if he'd just kissed a casket, bent over, giving mouth-to-mouth to the antichrist. A lot of Baaloney, I say. This mystic's gone Baalistic. And now a muddy quatrain from a Real True Believer:

> A face half-milky calm
> Half-scales, half-beehive,
> As the Red One practices feints
> On the black bull named Fido.

### Translation:

*At the year's midpoint, beneath a full moon a woman scales a large tuna while her son dances in a red cape with the family dog. Beware the coming of the Evil One!*

Bonehead! Son of a bonehead! Grandson of a charismatic! The next sound you hear will be old Mr. Beelzebub clearing his cancerous throat: Aaaaaaaargh! . . .

# Johannes Kepler

I'm moored to my La-Z-Boy, a book of astronomy in hand, the rudder of my unheavenly ship broken (read "heart" for "rudder," blockheads). You're being punished for crushing my tinfoil replica of Mother Earth with a basketball. I hear you moving upstairs, dodging tiny glow-in-the-dark stars falling from your ceiling. You think my astronomical theories stink. Even the Big Questions bore you. To be honest, I'm just curious why my ass has dropped. Let's consult a wise man . . . Much not to like about Kepler. Tormented by classmates, smelling like a donkey, he's awaiting the music of the spheres. We come upon him beating a note-book of Tycho Brahe with an ancient spyglass. "Be good to my bird," he chirps, trying to shake the celestial cacophony from his head. He's being held hostage by a circle, so you toss him a lovebird's elliptical egg, and . . . Eureka! Weeks later, passing out opiates, he warns of our imminent impact on the moon's surface. "Our bodies will roll themselves into balls," he says, "as spiders do, and we'll carry them by means of our will alone." Next thing, we're up to our ankles in moon dust, a star flaming by, borne on the back of a white dwarf. Kepler dons the mirrored, wrap-around sunglasses you've brought him; I display a snapshot of Galileo's middle finger preserved in a marble and glass case. "It's like a baseball trophy," you explain, and he nods warily, dropping the sunglasses low on his nose, breaking into a crazy dance as the Universe's Greatest Hits play on.

# Cotton Mather

Mather says, "I'm going to Entertain you with a Discourse." Yet another Wise Man, another Holy Man. But we need more than a fat Preface right now, more than a manly Sermon. Mather appears constipated, as if trying to pass a Chicken Bone. Another Refractory Child has gotten into his Brain. Meaning you, dearest Son. He's testing the Air with a Holy Hand, asking, "What Terriblest Thing has brought Ye here?" I could suggest your headless Nostradamus Puppet stuffed with old Playmates of the Month, or your Untamed Tongue. But I settle on a Seventeenth-century Misdemeanor. "I came upon him tormenting his Latin Book, yea, beating it with a Shoe, yea, a Work Boot." "There's no Ambidextering when it comes to the Devil," he says, even as you Pillow him with Palaver, try to set Fire to his Heart's goodliest Forest. "He doth saith prettily," Mather concedes, then that Look again, his Jaw out of Joint, yea, dropping to the Floor. He points to an Invisible Chain wrapped round your Neck—the Devil's Umbilical Cord, which he Grasps and Rides like a Broomstick, careening into the Fireplace, tossed back and forth as if by a Red-hot Hand. "Lord, let my Mouth show forth thy Praise," he cries. "Cursed be that Undutiful Absalom that makes Light of his Father." You duck, but seem unfazed, calmly cursing in lower-case punk Latin: *asinum meum basia, asinum meum basia . . .*

# Samuel Johnson

The 18th century, thank God there's still a God—Order, Design, Right Reason not yet gone left. "You're soooo Johnsonian," my wife says, handing me a yellow pill. I'm obsessing again, tearing clumps of hair from my head, besieging the lovebirds with a dried-out drumstick. Depression—laughter and hypochondria create such strange cozenage . . . We're slopping our way to the Café Voltaire, pooped from last night's cockfight and boxing matches, beer and gin afflicting us in a dreadful manner. "I'll have no more on't," I kept yelling, not quite sure what I meant. At the fair you befriended an Irishman who shattered a chamber pot by barking Greek phrases from Sappho. Prostitutes mud-wrestling, fannies spanked with birch rods, then to the inoculation party where we drank cockroach tea while soaking our testicles in warm vinegar. "Not the lessons I wanted you to learn," I say, feeding a half-eaten tomato to a one-legged dog. Let me repeat: We're slopping our way to the Café Voltaire, sucking in coal dust, up to our ankles in uric mud, passing a ballad singer, an apple vendor, a dead horse. "By your leave," a fancy-pants personage apologizes, his black sedan nearly running me down. Later, I tell Johnson I'm homesick, but he offers this explanation: "Long intervals of pleasure dissipate attention and weaken constancy." And how right he is! "Wastrel, Johnny Boy Esquire the Third, do you hear the words of this great depressed man? Do you recognize your likeness in his eyes?" But you're drunk again, cursing out a kidney pie in pig Latin. I look to Johnson for solace, but he's laughing, pinching wheat-stained vermin from under my wig, soberly addressing one at close range. "And thee," he says, "I shall name Boswell."

# Sade

The lovebirds are sleeping, exhausted from their failed attempts to make love. *Erosphere:* "The Definitive Adult Magazine"—"private lingerie modeling," "golden showers," "switchblade domination." You should be watching Home Run Derby, reading biographies of Richard the Lion-Hearted, doing one-arm pushups. "According to the Marquis," you say, "'nothing that causes an erection is villainous.'" Tell that to Justine. *Little Known Fact About the Marquis de Sade:* at Charenton Asylum everyone called him Dr. Sphincter. I tell thee, nocky boy, he was no more than a fat whiner. And where was the poetry? Not "her bannocks were like wheaten cakes"; not even, "unworthy to loosen the leather thongs of her studded bra." Just a guy with a zero and an exclamation point humping in his head, his penis dangling like an artificial leg. Old Sade Sack sulking in a cell, writing a play for an inmate who's carrying the child of John the Baptist. He doesn't even have a title. "How about 'Fetish Fair Fleamarket?'" you suggest, bowing from the waist. "How about 'Bi-Curious, Anal Housewives Want It Now?'"

# Darwin

Charles, we collect beetles too, red ants, horseflies, even tomato worms. But I like my bees in a bottle, my bulbs basketed. And why are we here, my beamish boy? "The sight of a naked savage in his native land is an event which can never be forgotten." Charles wrote that by lamplight as he watched fireflies jitterbug on the horizon. He saw God in a sea hedgehog, in an orchid, then a theory appeared, sudden and frightening as a new planet. It must have been difficult to kill God, like hugging a porcupine, like being bitten on the tongue by a dung beetle. "I am not an animal, I am a plant," you laugh—a remark dumb enough to renew my interest in self-fertilization . . . We're docked off the cliffs of Patagonia, fighting over the name of our new lovebird. You want to call him "Tupac," I like *"Dasein."* Charles has no idea what we're talking about. Later, he's climbing a chaos of rocks, extracting bits of seashells from a cliff. Sea creatures in the mountains? How did it all start? "Perhaps a great egg came forth," you offer, peeling off your "Gotta Sweat!" T-shirt. I say to picture God as a tone-deaf, handsome accordion player clinging hopelessly to his failed lounge act. And your cruel response? "Another useless metaphor from the Incredible Shrinking Penis." Which makes Charles laugh, no doubt thinking he'd like to see such a phenomenon, perhaps probe it with a sharp needle.

# Mary Shelley

The Villa Diodati, when vegetation rioted on earth at the mere hip-hop of a harp, and the genital spirit was more than just a medium-rare idea. I give two thumbs down to angry love, I give it an Everlasting Nay! "So dramatic," you say. You're boasting how you've discovered "Woman," so consider this question: "When a virgin marries a river, who plays at the reception?" Love is like this, my boy. We talk of young girls with red ponytails, slurping from pink champagne glasses impaled with tiny orange umbrellas. "Be not, let not, take heed," I warn. "Do not beat me with your heart-shaped club, your silly ideas, half-distinguished and persistent as a procession of ants. . . ." The Villa Diodati where everyone is sick of Byron, even the Monster. "Her smile, how persuasive it was, and how pathetic!" That's Percy. "If you were to have someone whip you, whom would you choose?" That's Byron. "I will be a good girl and never vex you more." That's Mary. How we'd like to hear those words, at night, in the study by candlelight. She's a woman with a mind, no slight blot on this Promethean landscape where every man is hung like a centaur, or thinks he is. Let's peek in on Sleeping Mary, dreaming of groves and corpses, of young Victor crouched over his creation, of the Villa Diodati itself, where tomorrow the Monster will once again lurch from her pen, while Shelley's and Byron's "I" and "Me" wrestle into the early morning hours.

# Houdini

"Houdinize: to release or extricate oneself from confinement, as by wriggling out." You've certainly mastered that trick, your every alibi a Trunk Mysterioso. Harry never made excuses. Instead—hard work, repetition . . . A Dime Museum: you're cracking yellow croquet balls on your cranium, trying to make a diamond materialize in a Big Mac; I'm scraping gold sequins off the floor with a dislocated big toe. And Harry? He's hanging upside down, inch-long needles dangling from his eyelids. "Behold, a miracle!" he shouts, then wants to know just what the hell a Big Mac is, and why we're here. "It was a bad winter, Harry: frozen birds smashing into failing gutters, our St. Bernard casting off its root-beer barrel and chasing two old cats. Then a fiendish hand crashed through the Great Beyond and grabbed me by the chi-chis." Which, of course, makes everyone laugh. Even the Dog-Faced Boy. But Harry's up for the challenge. He crawls into a large milk can. Much mumbling and banging, then a solution signaled by the moan of a conch shell. He leaps from the can, naked from the waist up, sweating, his eyes gun-metal grey. "Beware the Kalends of July!" he shouts. "Beware anyone even using the word Kalends!" And he's deadly serious. Later, sitting on a trick coffin in a cream-colored straitjacket, he's fed chunks of sirloin by the Bird Girl. "My whole life," he says, "I've been chasing the sound of my mother's heartbeat." Inside the ebony box, a woman is weeping.

# Freud

"If it weren't for pickpockets, Sigmund wouldn't have any sex life at all."

*That's* not funny, *that's* not original. "Unsatisfactory Citizenship." A No. 12 on your report card. *That's* not funny, either. Or smoking pot. Or bookmarking G-spots on the Internet. I swear, if you snuck outside to fart, the wind would blow it back in . . . Sigmund, You the Man. A little help, please. Cure this Oedipal itch, marinade this meathead . . . Freud, old and quiet, sipping from a whitebone coffee mug adorned with the image of the Sphinx. He's mourning a lost dream, picking a piece of lint from his beard. Nearby, the famous couch covered with an oriental rug. I can smell its horsehair stuffing, I can smell his cigar. "Humbaba, Humbaba," you mumble, attracting his attention with a Gilgameshic mantra. You plan to manufacture a key ring in the shape of a brooch bearing the face of this bearded old man. "Humbaba, Humbaba." *"That's* not funny, either," I say, then get distracted by a flamboyant entrance. It's Wilhelm Fliess, alias Chard deNose, commissioned to explore your *corpora cavernosa,* a phrase you'd understand if you ever flashed your flash cards. "Ain't got no biorhythms," you laugh, "ain't got no self-control. Can't even dance." But Fliess will have none of it. He has you strapped to the couch, giving you a fascist facial, poking at a mound of nasal flesh with a sharp scalpel. "I'll give you Humbaba," he says, as Freud looks on, toying with a thick piece of gauze.

# Einstein

Albert said: "Our situation on this earth seems strange," and I surely second that emotion. You say, "I want to be like . . . . . . Albert." And who wouldn't. To have a head naturally swollen with B-12. So nice to say, "That woman is a violin," and watch people perk up, listen. Yet did you know his grandmother vomited when she first saw him? It was that same head, as big as a watermelon. No wonder he didn't speak for three years. He was fixed on the face of a compass, entombed in an imaginary spacecraft exiting our galaxy's backside. None of his pegs fit . . . Contrasts between you and Albert: Albert was saddened at the regimented motions of soldiers; you're aroused by twelve one-arm pushups; Albert blushed at the marriage of a curved line and falling apple, at a star without compassion; you're starstruck by a little girl in pink hot pants; Albert compared fame to "feeding time at the zoo"; you want to broadcast your pimple picking on the Internet; Albert . . . "Would you please please please stop talking?" Nocky boy, all he wanted was to see God, to spend his life straightening out one enormous paper clip. Which is where we find him in his old straw hat and rumpled white suit. He looks up, and we await another grave statement from another Great Man. "I'm with the boy," is all he says.

# Hitler

War club, tomahawk, scalping knife! Bayonet, machine gun, Luger! Brainchildren of brains quartered then wrongly reassembled. Hitler-as-child. That's what interests us. No wise-guy stuff. Not "The camera loves your face, Adolf." Not "Everything went well until tea was served." The village of Hafeld at the base of the Salzkammergut mountains, Adolf's father trudging down a path, cloaked in bees. Adolf on a cemetery wall, gazing up at stars. Or in an apple tree, waving his arms, pretending to be a weathervane, a watchman, a thresher. A besotted barefoot shepherd enters his sights, his finger tapping an imaginary trigger. "I am great! I am marvelous!" the sky turning a hectic red, tall tales of Old Shatterhand sprouting like jagged stalks of lightning. Nearby a bull calf lies all atwitter. Which is how it starts— an unthinkable idea popped cleanly from its socket, then you turn to see the dragon's followed you home. "Just one question," you say, grabbing him by the throat. "Just one damn question." On hot summer days villagers say Adolf held conversations with windblown trees, painted his lips with raspberry juice.

But all we see are his war club, tomahawk, scalping knife!

# Hemingway

I was writing a play called *Nada*. You were interested in "Grace under pressure," thinking it was a sex act. "Papa, do you mind if I call you Daddy?" Which, of course, is a tautology—a word Hemingway would've hated, along with "favonian" and "phocine," though they were good enough for Vladimir N. . . . Pamplona! The running of the bulls. "Airnesto?" I say, with a phony Andalusian accent. He's standing in the middle of a two-room flat, wearing tan shorts and a blood-red apron with "Born to Fish" etched in white. I'm leaning out a window, glaring down at a posse of hungover aficionados, red hoof prints, like birthmarks, staining their backs. Yesterday, for a brief moment, everyone was a pugilist. "Someday," Ernesto says, "someone will place a gun in my hand and say, 'Follow your instincts.' Meanwhile, can't eat, can't drink, can't fuck." "But you're a good cook," I say. And he is! This Ernesto is an old Ernesto—his thin white hair combed forward, his love-horn filed and shaved down like that of a half-bull. "I say, we all could use one of those wiry ballbusters you wrote about, some freckled-face, redheaded expatriate who'll appear at the front door, swearing like a storm trooper and hugging a weatherbeaten wine flask." He smiles, then grabs a live ten-inch trout from a metal pail, knocking it unconscious with a head butt. Suddenly, the twang of an acoustic guitar, and you enter from the bathroom, naked except for a hand towel the size of a fig leaf. You're delirious with fever, half-believing you've been bull-wounded. "Jasmine's neck has finally healed from the bite of that German shepherd," you announce, which comment piques this here picador—meaning me. But Ernesto seems elated, throws the wet trout against a whiskey-stained wall. "Antonio, Antonio," he moans, removing his red apron, making an artful pass at you.

# Malcolm X

"White America is doomed!" Finally, a statement we agree with.

"If I were black, I know I'd be angry." "You're always angry, anyway," you say. And I am. I am the angriest white man in America. I shoot people the finger for adjusting their rearview mirrors, I curse into the ears of telemarketers . . . Mid-twentieth century, Malcolm's eighth grade teacher patronizing him: "You've got to be realistic about being a nigger, Malcolm." And Malcolm thinks: *By any means necessary!* . . . Two blocks down, our resident skinhead rearranges his collection of human skulls, says he can prove white superiority by measuring the distance between his navel and penis. "I am the reincarnation of Hitler," he announces. "I come from the planet Zeno." And Malcolm says, *By any means necessary!* And: *When people are angry, they are not interested in logic, they are not interested in odds, they are not interested in consequences.* Jimmy Reed was angry, just back from Nam with pink pills, blue pills, white pills, all wrapped in a ball of tinfoil. One night two tons of steel rods dropped from his overhead crane. "Maybe he wasn't angry," you say, "maybe just tired." And now, ladies and gentleman, time for a few white, liberal anecdotes—about your one black friend who took you to your first rap concert ("dog, it was phat"); about your one black friend who dated your sister ("he was a gentleman"); about your one black friend you got drunk with under a midnight sky brightened by sparks from the steel plant ("he called me Brother"). "White, blue-eyed devil." "Two-legged snake." "White ape and beast." We are all of these—even you, my tow-headed, green-eyed gangsta boy, with a black, silk bandanna around your head, lip-syncing lyrics of a Wu-Tang song predicting your doom.

When Malcolm was shot, some cops were sleeping, others playing three-card monte in the men's room. *By any means necessary!* Malcolm would have shouted.

# Maharishi Yogi

I have a mantra. It sounds like αἱμά, the Greek word for blood. I want to be a swami but I talk too much. I mean to say, I don't listen, I cut people off. Last week my main chakra was out of whack—rattling like a tambourine. My *Fana* was famished. When someone says, "The true seeing is when there is no seeing," I get a headache. Tomorrow I'll change my mantra to *But,* yours to *Yet.* At least then we'll be honest. I'd break Descartes' kneecaps if I could, he's the real troublemaker. So very loud in his Land of Self—opposites rubbing shoulders, chanting, or doing a sexy dance. "Manure worm." "Navel Gazer." We gladly embrace these insults. "I exhale next to plants," you laugh. "I do my best to stay poor." For that wisecrack, I proclaim you my Sherpa companion. You will be in charge of my yak herd. Your new name will be Chucklehead.

    Master: *The dead will return in taxi cabs.*

    Disciple: *But, Master, there are no taxi cabs in Khembalung.*

    Master: *Which is why the dead will return.*

I'm getting better at this. Yesterday, I sat still for an hour. I took twenty minutes to pee. It was a kind of meditation.

# Return

End of the twentieth century and I'm still angry. The new hero same as the old hero. And the poets? They're out back wrestling in the wet mulch, writing each other love letters with bird shit on brown paper bags. Just want to don my pajamas and curl up with a good book, but there aren't any. "Take it easy, Lady Philosophy," you warn. "Whoa there, Mr. Negativity." You're pointing to your souvenirs: jodhpurs from Jodhpur, an artificial ass from the court of Louis XIV, an eyelash of Catherine the Great. I shave my head, put on my swim cap limed with Bengay. I sit in a corner, sifting through the ashes of famous people. It's a metaphor, gentle reader. It's not a metaphor, gentle reader. Like everyone else, we wanted to become a legend, or a footnote to an obscure anecdote. We were driven by the certainty of heavy soil and that starlet's buttocks. And I wanted to Educate you, and would have, if the cockroaches hadn't eaten our canoe. There was certainly no ostriching on my part; I faced down every truth, every falsehood. "On my trip I met a woman named DNA," you croon, with that silly look on your face, then ask to play outside with the Famous Poet, who's holding a sacred fish over his head, saying, "When the hook is caught in the lower jaw that means your *vahine* has been unfaithful." This is not a metaphor, gentle reader. Not even a Strange Fact of the Week. Just a little jab to keep us moving, to keep us on the run.

# About the Author

Peter Johnson is founder and editor of *The Prose Poem: An International Journal*, and editor of *The Best of The Prose Poem: An International Journal* (White Pine Press, 2000). His books of prose poems include *Pretty Happy!* (White Pine Press, 1997), and *Love Poems for the Millennium* (Quale Press, 1998). His collection of short stories, *I'm a Man*, won Raincrow Press' 1997 Fiction Chapbook Contest, and in 1999 he was awarded a creative writing fellowship from the National Endowment for the Arts. He is also a contributing editor and featured writer on *Web del Sol*. Born and raised in Buffalo, New York, he currently teaches at Providence College in Providence, Rhode Island, where he resides with his wife and son.

*Acknowledgments (continued)*

*North Dakota Quarterly:* "London" and "Cotton Mather"
*Quarterly West:* "Home," "Tex-Mex," "Transylvania," "Berlin," and "New York"
*Silverfish Review:* "Bombay," "Palm Springs," and "Geneva"
*Third Coast:* "Scotland"
*Untitled:* "Mary Shelley" and "Houdini"
*Verse:* "Hong Kong," "Moscow," "Oslo," "Hemingway," "Maharishi Yogi,"
    and "Return"
*Web del Sol:* "Sade," "Darwin," "Freud," and "Einstein"

I wish to thank Chard deNiord, Russell Edson, Todd Gernes, Brian Johnson, P. H. Liotta, Gian Lombardo, Elaine LaMattina, and Walker Rumble, all of whom saved me from embarrassment with their specific suggestions. I also thank the National Endowment for the Arts, whose generous support gave me both time and clarity of mind to write many of these prose poems. Finally, a special thanks to R. Newell Elkington who designed this book.